Wild Women

Celebrate the wild woman in yourself! Let the women in
these pages serve as your inspiration, your mentors, your
tutors in the fine art of being exuberantly female. Their
words may very well empower you to write your own
stories, thoughts, dreams . . . and more.

In this journal, you will find puckish quips, profound
declarations, and penetrating insights from women in
every walk of life. What do they all have in common?
Merely—and marvelously—that way of getting right to the
point that makes Wild Women so much fun to be around.
So go ahead and embrace their attitude—you're in the
best (and wildest!) of company!

10
ways to be a
Wild Woman

---

1. Keep in touch with your inner rebel. (It's okay if the relationship is merely friendly rather than hot and heavy—we can't all be Madonna or Susan B. Anthony!)

2. Try to act in a way that is true to your deepest self, even if your mother, significant other, or society in general does not support your behavior. (Easier said than done . . . but highly gratifying in the long run.)

3. Befriend and nurture other women.

4. Befriend and nurture yourself.

5. Speak up! Silence is deadly boring—and sometimes just plain deadly. Pouring out your passion in letters, e-mails, or manifestos is a fine alternative if you're not the type to scale that soapbox in public.

6. Learn as much as you can about women in history. The more you know about the accomplishments of others, the more inspired you will feel to challenge the status quo.

7. Take pride in women who defy, exceed, or trifle with conventional expectations.

8. Take one step (even a baby one) each week to promote a truly female-friendly environment in your home, community, nation, or the world at large.

9. Raise a little (or a lot of), um, heck . . . whenever and wherever the need arises.

10. In the immortal words of Red Hot Mama Sophie Tucker: "Keep breathing!"

"Surviving is important, but thriving is *elegant*."

—Maya Angelou

"How many cares one loses when one decides not to be something, but to be someone."
-Gabrielle "Coco" Chanel

"I don't want to make money. I just want to be wonderful."
                                                              -Marilyn Monroe

"Don't agonize. Organize."
-Florynce Kennedy

"I resent the idea that you can't be both sexy and smart. When I dyed my hair, the peroxide didn't fry my brain cells."
-Loni Anderson

"I used to want the words "She tried" on my tombstone. Now I want "She did it."
-Katherine Dunham

"When I think about my life, I am sure I will not arrive at an old age.
But I would rather sing one day as a lion than a hundred years as a sheep."

-Cecelia Bartoli

"Liberty is a better husband than love to many of us."

-Louisa May Alcott

"A sheltered life can be a daring life as well. For all serious daring starts from within."
-Eudora Welty

"I don't eat junk foods and I don't think junk thoughts."
-Peace Pilgrim

"If women ruled the world and

we all got massages,

there would be no war."

–Carrie Snow

"For every hero in this world, there's at least one shero."
—Johnetta B. Cole

"The only sin is mediocrity."
-Martha Graham

"Live each moment as if your hair is on fire!"
-Suzannah B. Troy

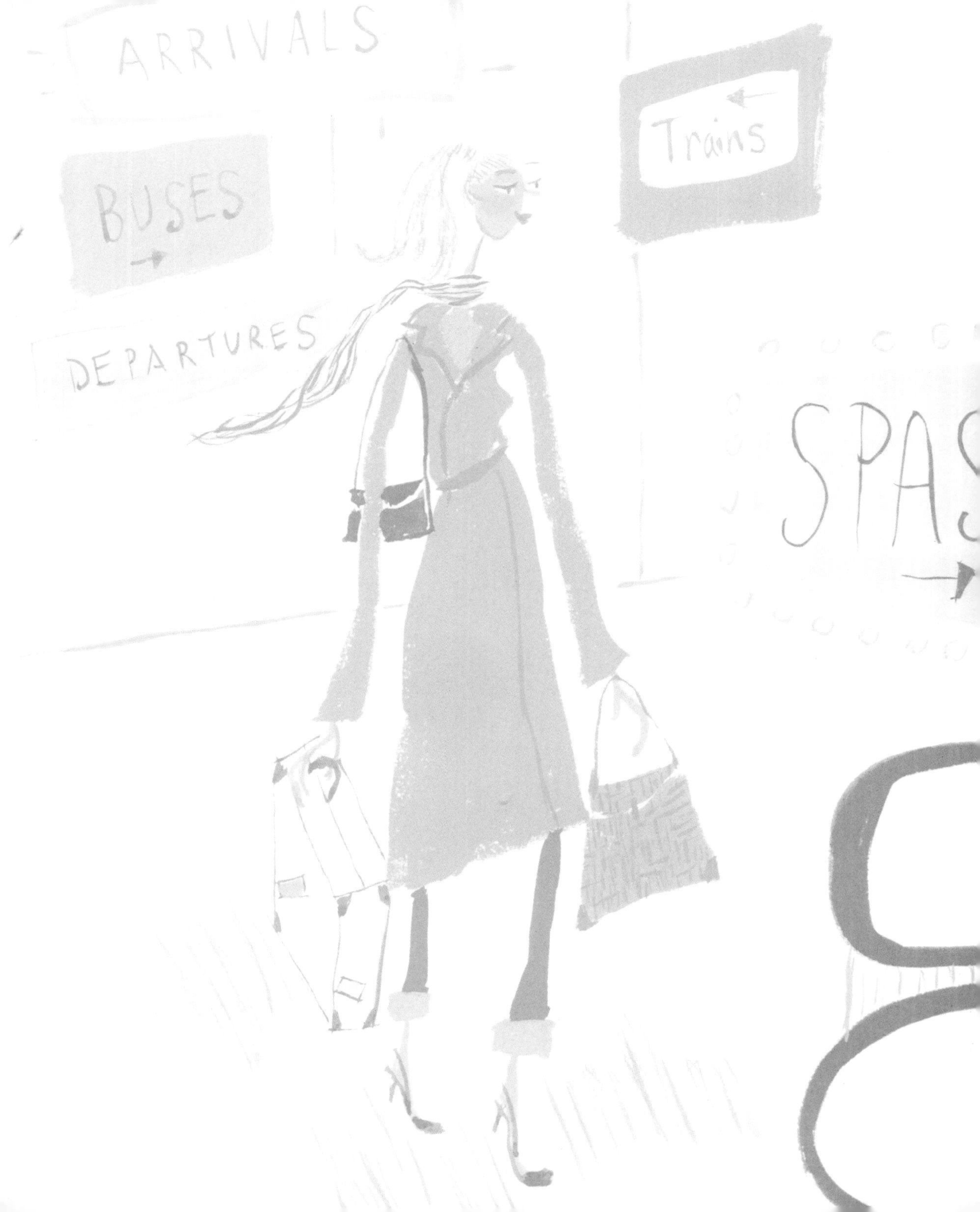
ARRIVALS
BUSES
Trains
DEPARTURES
SPAS

"I believe the second half of one's life is meant to be better than the first half. The first half is finding out how you do it. And the second half is enjoying it."
-Frances Lear

"I have the same goal I've had ever since I was a girl. I want to rule the world."

-Madonna

"Good girls go to heaven, bad girls go everywhere."
-Helen Gurley Brown

"I've never had a humble opinion.

If you've got an opinion, why

be humble about it?"

—Joan Baez

"We don't see things as they are, we see them as we are."
—Anaïs Nin

"When women are depressed they either eat or go shopping. Men invade another country. It's a whole different way of thinking."
-Elayne Boosler

"When people keep telling you that you can't do a thing,
you kind of like to try it."
-Margaret Chase Smith

"Life itself

is the proper binge."

–Julia Child

"Time and trouble will tame an advanced young woman, but an advanced old woman is uncontrollable by any earthly force."
-Dorothy Sayers

"When I was 40, I used to wonder what people thought of me. Now I wonder what *I* think of them."
-Brooke Astor

"At the worst, a house unkept cannot be so distressing as a life unlived."
-Rose Macaulay

"It's only the best fruit the birds pick at."

-Bette Davis

"I became a feminist as an alternative to becoming a masochist."
-Sally Kempton

"To love what you do

and feel that it matters—how could

anything be more fun?"

—Katharine Graham

"If a woman hasn't met the right man by the time she's 24, she may be lucky."
-Deborah Kerr

"My weight is always perfect for my height—which varies."

-Nicole Hollander

"I am too pretty to bother with an eyebrow pencil."
-Chao Luan-Luan

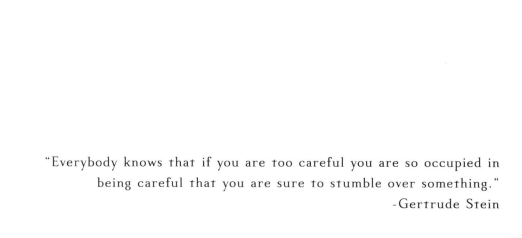

"Everybody knows that if you are too careful you are so occupied in
being careful that you are sure to stumble over something."
-Gertrude Stein

Take pride in women who

defy, exceed, or trifle

with conventional expectations.

"I have never wanted to be a man. I have often wanted to be effective as a woman but I never thought that trousers would do the trick."
-Eleanor Roosevelt

"In time your relatives will come to accept the idea that
a career is as important to you as your family. Of
course, in time the polar ice cap will melt."
-Barbara Dale

"I am a marvelous housekeeper. Every time I leave a man I keep his house."

-Zsa Zsa Gabor

"The roosters may crow, but the hens deliver the goods."

-Ann Richards

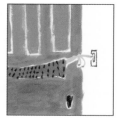

"It is better to be a bad original than a good copy."
-The Marquise du Defand

"When I look at myself, I am so beautiful, I scream with joy."
-Maria Montez